Construction Machines

Backhoe Loaders

Dash!
LEVELED READERS
An Imprint of Abdo Zoom • abdobooks.com

2

2

Dash!
LEVELED READERS

Level 1 – Beginning
Short and simple sentences with familiar words or patterns for children who are beginning to understand how letters and sounds go together.

Level 2 – Emerging
Longer words and sentences with more complex language patterns for readers who are practicing common words and letter sounds.

Level 3 – Transitional
More developed language and vocabulary for readers who are becoming more independent.

abdobooks.com

Published by Abdo Zoom, a division of ABDO, PO Box 398166, Minneapolis, Minnesota 55439. Copyright © 2019 by Abdo Consulting Group, Inc. International copyrights reserved in all countries. No part of this book may be reproduced in any form without written permission from the publisher. Dash!™ is a trademark and logo of Abdo Zoom.

Printed in the United States of America, North Mankato, Minnesota.
092018
012019

Photo Credits: iStock, Shutterstock
Production Contributors: Kenny Abdo, Jennie Forsberg, Grace Hansen, John Hansen
Design Contributors: Dorothy Toth, Neil Klinepier

Library of Congress Control Number: 2018945597

Publisher's Cataloging in Publication Data

Names: Murray, Julie, author.
Title: Backhoe loaders / by Julie Murray.
Description: Minneapolis, Minnesota : Abdo Zoom, 2019 | Series: Construction machines | Includes online resources and index.
Identifiers: ISBN 9781532125126 (lib. bdg.) | ISBN 9781641856577 (pbk) | ISBN 9781532126147 (ebook) | ISBN 9781532126659 (Read-to-me ebook)
Subjects: LCSH: Diggers--Juvenile literature. | Construction equipment--Juvenile literature. | Machinery--Construction--Juvenile literature.
Classification: DDC 624.152--dc23

Table of Contents

Backhoe Loaders 4

Different Jobs 8

More Facts 22

Glossary 23

Index 24

Online Resources 24

Backhoe Loaders

A backhoe loader is important at construction sites. It can handle many different jobs.

It is two machines in one!
It has a loader bucket on
the front. On the other
side is a backhoe.

Different Jobs

Backhoe loaders can dig, load, level, and carry.

The driver sits in the cab. The seat can turn 360 degrees. The driver controls both sides of the machine.

The loader is in front of the cab. It is used to scoop and carry. The loader can level dirt and sand too.

The backhoe is in back of the cab. It is used for digging. It has a **boom**, an arm, and a bucket.

The **boom** is like an upper arm.
The arm moves like a forearm.
The bucket digs, scoops, and
holds like a hand!

The driver must park the machine to use the backhoe. Two **stabilizer** legs keep it from moving.

A backhoe loader is small and **versatile**. It is used at lots of construction jobs!

21

More Facts

- The first serial backhoe loader was made in 1957. It was the CASE Model 320.

- JCB GT is the fastest backhoe loader in the world. It has a top speed of 72.58 mph (116.8 kph).

- Today, backhoe loaders cost between $20,000 - $150,000. The cost depends on the size.

Glossary

boom – the long arm that moves left and right and connects the arm and bucket to the main body of the machine.

stabilizer – the device that keeps the machine from rolling or being unstable.

versatile – able to do many different things well.

Index

backhoe 7, 15, 19

boom 15, 16

bucket 7, 15, 16

cab 10, 15

driver 10, 19

loader 7, 13

parts 7

size 21

uses 9, 13, 15, 16, 19, 21

Online Resources

Booklinks
NONFICTION NETWORK
FREE! ONLINE NONFICTION RESOURCES

To learn more about backhoe loaders, please visit **abdobooklinks.com**. These links are routinely monitored and updated to provide the most current information available.